TAROT DEL TORO

A Tarot Deck and Guidebook Inspired by the World of Guillermo del Toro

FOREWORD BY
GUILLERMO DEL TORO

WRITTEN AND ILLUSTRATED BY
TOMÁS HIJO

TITAN BOOKS

AN INSIGHT EDITIONS BOOK

"Any legend, any creature, any symbol we ever stumble on already exists in a vast cosmic reservoir where archetypes wait. Shapes looming outside our Platonic cave. We naturally believe ourselves clever and wise, so advanced, and those who came before us so naive and simple ... when all we truly do is echo the order of the universe, as it guides us."

—THE FALL

CONTENTS

Foreword 6

Introduction 8

What is Tarot? 10

The Major Arcana 13

The Minor Arcana 58

   The Court Cards Interpreted 60

   Numerical Cards 76

Readings 78

Final Word 86

FOREWORD

My mother read the Tarot to anyone that would ask her—regardless of the time or setting. She always carried her deck of cards, nested in a velvet pouch inside her handbag, and treated with great care and respect. The edges of the cards were worn and stained from the frequency and familiarity of their handling.

Throughout my childhood, she taught me to read the I-Ching (wrongly, it turns out, but I corrected that later) and the tea leaves and a bit of palmistry . . . but she neglected to teach me the Tarot. As it happens, she would, finally, decades later—as we found ourselves trapped in a small hotel during a Hurricane in the South Pacific.

The archetypes locked in the Tarot are pliable, multivalent; they mutate according to the card laid beside them. They spell one fate right side up and the opposite upside down. An unexpected turn is always one card away and, in that, the Tarot is like life itself. Cyphered in here are centuries of Hermetic knowledge and symbols. These cards tap into primordial, totemic things.

If you believe that our acts and ourselves have not only a tangible meaning, but a symbolic one, then you understand how symbols are both intimate and universal. As James Joyce puts it: ". . . We walk through ourselves, meeting robbers, ghosts, giants, old men, young men, wives, widows, brothers-in-love, but always meeting ourselves . . ."

Symbols tap to the cosmic root of our being—that which is hardwired in all of us, so we can exist in harmony or chaos within the vastness of our Universe.

I started to use the Tarot not only as a storytelling device, but to hone my storytelling intuition, to offer nimble combinations and possible outcomes for characters or dramatic arcs. Oftentimes, the cards would suggest ideas that seemed improbable or foolish, but also unfettered, liberating.

No matter what way you use these cards—you will always be having a dialogue with yourself. Shuffling and turning the Tarot while pondering life's questions connects the cards to a greater matrix and the most intimate one.

What you have in your hands now is a gateway to the largest truths and an infinite matrix of stories, insight, and fate.

Tomás Hijo is, in my estimation, one of the great modern engravers. His work is vital; modern, but steeped in a grand tradition. We have taken great care in marrying the Arcana with the characters and symbols of my filmography. Tomás has carefully composed each card, he has selected a color palette that mimics that of most decks, and has given us a Deck full of miniature works of art.

But he has also made sure that they work as a system—that they render for you the experience you may seek.

There are only twelve musical notes, and with them, we have written every song there is. The Major Arcana almost doubles that number, and it will surely guide you into knowing thyself and accessing the Universe within.

As above, so below-

Guillermo del Toro
Los Angeles, 2020

INTRODUCTION

During the summer of 2018, Guillermo invited me to have dinner in a Japanese restaurant in Paris. We ate sushi and talked about a million things. I don't know how tarot came up, but the idea thundered into my head with its definitive title perfectly formed: "Why don't we make the Tarot del Toro?" Guillermo stared at me and said, "¡Órale!" which means, "Go ahead!" I didn't need to explain that I was imagining a deck inhabited by his creations. I can still feel the emotion of that special moment when two of my greatest passions merged into a single project.

When I returned home, I visited Don Miguel. He is an authority among esoteric practitioners in my hometown of Salamanca and the best tarot reader I have ever met. He is the person who showed me what tarot is and who taught me how to read it. A tarot with images taken from movies? Don Miguel didn't like the idea. Who was I to alter the perfect images of the mystical deck? According to him, the Tarot de Marseilles is perfect, and any change would destroy its power. I explained to him that I had thought deeply about the project and confirmed that Guillermo's work miraculously connected with Don Miguel's beloved cards. I promised that Tarot del Toro would not be one of those decks that forgot the symbolic power of the old cards.

Don Miguel went blind a long time before the first Guillermo del Toro film was shot—therefore he had not seen any of his work. I decided to sit by his side, open my laptop in front of us, and play Guillermo's films one by one. We spent hours that way, and I enjoyed explaining to him every shot and scene. When a motif Guillermo and I were thinking of using appeared on the screen, I grew enthusiastic. "Don Miguel, this monster with the iron hand will be Strength!" Or, "I'll use this bomb instead of the angel of Judgement!" Don Miguel overcame his reticence very quickly and did not hesitate to propose his own ideas that went, to my surprise, further and further from the literality of tarot. "Is that housemaid holding a knife? She is your valet of Blades." Or, "Human fetuses floating in jars of liquor? There he is. The Hanged."

I designed and carved every card, and when I finished, I was able to show them to him. All my engravings are deeply embossed, so Don Miguel was able to "see" them through his fingers. I am proud to declare that he approved of every card and became, at times, greatly enthusiastic.

As a final gift, Don Miguel recommended his own way to read the cards and gave me permission to share it with you. Everything is included at the end of the book.

And what about Guillermo? Guillermo followed the creation of every card from the sketch to its final form, suggested wonderful ideas, and helped me to overcome some obstacles that arose. I can't conceive what combination of tarot cards could show the inconceivable amount of good luck I have had by having such wonderful people by my side. I hope this deck brings you as much joy and insight as it has to me.

WHAT IS TAROT?

"Symbols are lovingly inlaid to add to a second or third reading, and even to change radically if you combine them. Symbols have that capacity; they are not ciphers that remain immutable."

—GUILLERMO DEL TORO

The tarot is a deck of illustrated cards used for the purposes of self-discovery and divination. Many different models exist, each featuring different images and card combinations. Despite this variation, almost all decks are made up of two groups of cards: the Major and Minor Arcana. The Major Arcana features twenty-two cards illustrated with classic spiritual symbology, allegorical scenes, and archetypal characters. The Minor Arcana comprises four groups of cards, called suits, each of which bears a distinctive symbol. In this deck, the four suits are Wands, Goblets, Discs, and Blades. Each suit is made up of fourteen cards. Ten of them are numbered starting with the ace, and four show courtly figures: a king, a queen, a knight, and a valet.

The origin of the tarot deck—and the magical practices and games related to it—are unknown. Some eighteenth-century scholars such as Court de Gébelin and Etteilla stated that tarot was the Book of Thoth, written only seventeen years after the universal flood. Others assert it was the Moors who introduced tarot while doing business with the merchants of present-day Italy. Others refute these theories and propose a Chinese origin or an Indian birthplace similar to the figures of chess. Others propose theories about Hebrew Kabbalists or Cathar heretics looking for a way to express their forbidden doctrine.

Honestly, we don't know much more than that the cards existed by the twelfth century and were at least used for card games, if not for divination. There is proof of that in the many legal documents that tried to ban such games. Cards appear listed in many wills, suggesting that decks were very valuable. The invention of the printing press in the fifteenth century and the improvement of engraving techniques allowed the printing of cheaper decks, which became more and more popular.

It is not clear when tarot began to be used for divination, but it is undeniable that it has an inherent symbolic nature that invites us to do so. Some cards remind us of pagan gods, ancient figures of power, astrological elements, virtues, and other classic archetypes. Trying to find meaning in these symbols is a temptation that's hard to resist.

Nowadays, tarot is used for three purposes: an aid in self-exploration, a tool for predicting the future, and a source of inspiration in creating stories. All three objectives can be fulfilled at the same time. For many practitioners, tarot functions as a set of images with an open and interconnected symbolism. It is so well built that it allows us to see in the cards our desires, fears, and projections of our own identity. Whoever consults the cards—for themselves or for another person—is able to narrate a story drawn from real life to unravel motives, decipher issues, and reveal characters and their intentions.

With enough intuition, connections can be made and predictions laid out.

If you are a storyteller, tarot will answer the questions any story asks. Who is this character who has popped up in my head? How will this character act? What do I need to handle this situation? How should I go from here to there? Tarot cards have helped authors as varied as Italo Calvino, Alejandro Jodorowsky, John Steinbeck, and Stephen King to unfold their stories. Because there are infinite tales lurking inside the tarot cards.

Perhaps that is the true power of tarot: the creative and ritual use of the archetypes it includes. The power of symbols and human intuition. But we can't forget that, for many people, the mysterious energy—ancient Egyptian, Chinese, Kabbalistic, or Romani—that fuels tarot's magic is real magic. Who knows?

Use these cards freely, become familiar with their meaning and make them your own. Don't forget that they don't mean anything separately. They only reveal their true potential when read together. Accept the suggestions that bloom in your mind, even if they contradict the explanations in this book. Let the symbols speak to you.

Don't be afraid. You'll learn that neither the XIII card—the one with the skeleton—nor the Devil are exactly what they seem to be. And if at any moment, the cards tell you something frightening, remember the inscription on the door of the labyrinth from Guillermo's iconic fantasy movie *Pan's Labyrinth*: "In consiliis nostris, fatum nostrum est," which roughly translates to, "Our choices determine our fate." Cards can point in a direction, but—for better or for worse—only your steps will lead you there.

THE MAJOR ARCANA

THE FOOL

·THE FOOL·

The Fool is the only tarot card that is not numbered. Perhaps the reason is that it needs to be put aside. For many scholars, tarot is a path and the Fool not one of its steps, but the character who walks through it. According to this idea, we find a character with no previous identity. All possible paths unfold before him. From his wooden spoon hangs a minimal pack and a strange pet bug follows him. That bug—a mantis—

symbolizes instinct, and we can't be sure if it is a threat or a playmate.

In this deck, the Fool card is inspired by the faun from *Pan's Labyrinth*. The Fool, like the faun, is a primal being that can adopt the roles of both a jester and a mystical pilgrim. He can be a mysterious wanderer, a threatening intruder, or a frightened and lost child.

All these meanings develop—as with all the cards—depending on the position of the card, upright or inverted, and the cards that surround it. In personal matters, the Fool speaks of merry unconsciousness and lightness. When it appears inverted, it becomes the Lost One and speaks of disorientation and even dementia. In matters of love and friendship, it brings a certain lack of commitment, which is aggravated if it appears inverted. It almost never suggests a good capacity for business, unless it has to do with improvisation or sudden inspiration.

In the presence of the World, the Fool signifies a happy ending to a process; with card XIII, some transformative event; with the Wheel of Fortune, especially if inverted, the return to the starting point; with the Magician, the necessary preparation of the tools for the journey. In the presence of the Hanged, the pilgrim is blocked, paralyzed, or lost.

"The saddest journey in the world is the one that follows a precise itinerary. Then you're not a traveler. You're just a tourist."

—GUILLERMO DEL TORO

I THE MAGICIAN

The old French tarots call the Magician *Le Bateleur*, which means juggler, acrobat, or street performer. He is one who crafts wonders, the weaver of dreams, the alchemist. Of course, Tarot del Toro dedicates the Magician to Guillermo himself. In his hand and on his table, he displays the tools of his trade: the Cronos Device (a device of great transformative power), the miraculous mandrake from

Pan's Labyrinth, machine parts, an insect, and a razor blade—a recurrent element in his films and an homage to the master Luis Buñuel.

As in the classic tarots, these objects reference the four suits of the Minor Arcana: a blade, some goblets, a couple of discs, and the mandrake, representing the earthly power of the wands.

The Magician transforms spiritual energy into real-world change, and its appearance on a card spread speaks of creativity, originality, skill, and confidence. If it is related to relationships or emotions, it is a sign of potential success that indicates the existence of resources and capacities to undertake new projects.

The Chariot gives the Magician an extra dose of helpful initiative and drive. On the other hand, the Moon can push him into introspection, which can improve the creative work but prevent its dissemination. Along with the Emperor, the Magician can coordinate the efforts of a team of complementary creative people. With the Devil, he risks becoming an accursed artist.

Inverted, he becomes the Deceiver. In this position, the Magician relates to the trickster and fake artist who deceives others or deceives himself. He is the snake oil salesman or the victim of his ego. Or both.

"Hidden in every limitation lies an opportunity. And for every obstacle you face, there is a simple and perfect solution, creatively. And your work is to find it."

—Guillermo del Toro

II THE HIGH PRIESTESS

In many of the ancient tarots, this card represents the goddesses of the sacred mysteries. Throughout their many incarnations, the goddesses have been secret keepers with a passive stance toward the physical world. Tarot del Toro shows in this card the figure of Nuala, the elf princess from *Hellboy II*, who resonates beyond any doubt with this nature.

 Like the Magician, the High Priestess is a figure of creation and growth, but her nature is more reflective and mysterious, and her energy manifests itself in a subtler inward focus. Unlike the Magician, she sits quietly and seems to need only a scroll—which she does not even look at, as she already knows it—to channel her art. Her finest tools are secrecy and intuition. We see a veil behind her, which seems about to wrap itself around her head. This is a reference to the veil of Isis, which in the classics represented the impossibility of penetrating the secrets of nature. Hence the plant motif on the veil.

There are two more important symbols on this card. The dagger in the ground can be interpreted as a renunciation of direct action; and the egg, an alchemical and universal symbol enclosing the idea of secret and isolated creative power.

The High Priestess speaks of wisdom and insight, of turning your attention to intimate and secret matters. It always signifies growth for oneself and others, although it never manifests itself loudly or with quick results. The Sun can enlighten the High Priestess by making its revelations more powerful, perhaps even blinding if it appears reversed. Justice can make its presence especially beneficial to the social order. The Hermit at her side can transform her into a saint or a mystic. Combined with the Chariot or Strength, she can achieve a remarkable influence, and if the Devil or the Moon are around, we can find ourselves before the archetypes of the seductive sorceress or the witch who dances barefoot at the Sabbath.

When inverted, she is the Cloistered Nun, and she has lost her ability to channel her energy. She is a victim of her secrets and intuitions, and she sinks into passivity. Neurosis and depression can take hold and turn her into a sterile burden.

"Everything in our universe is ciphered, and to know the cipher is to know the thing—and to know the thing is to command it."

—THE FALL

III THE EMPRESS

The Empress is easy to define by its similarities to and differences from other cards. Like the High Priestess, she bears the idea of fertility; however, it is not a secret potential but a joyful motherhood. She has not an unhatched egg but a thriving and well-protected baby. She is also wise, but more practical, communicative, and warm. Like the Emperor, her husband, she holds power, but she does not make use of it in an authoritative way, rather spontaneously and naturally. While the Emperor seeks order and peace, the Empress looks for happiness and harmony. She is therefore a queen and a mother.

For this card, Tarot del Toro pictures a character inspired by one from *Pan's Labyrinth:* Carmen, Ofelia's mother, in her incarnation as the queen of the underworld realm. This is how the little girl sees her at the end of the story, with her brother asleep in her arms. The Empress is shown with wings because of her fairy nature and bears a scepter and a crown as symbols of her power. The eagle, another symbol of power, is displayed on her dress as opposed to on a shield as it is in the Tarot de Marseilles. Then again, perhaps it is not an eagle but the raven of wisdom.

The appearance of the Empress always speaks of natural leadership and warmth, of forces oriented toward germination, growth, and hope. As a symbol of motherhood, it can be understood in various ways. If next to the Moon, the Empress can grow obsessed with her maternal side and forget about herself. With the World, one can expect a perfect blooming of whatever has begun to grow. It is a very good card when related to social issues, especially if the Emperor is around, because together, these archetypes can bring all the necessary will and authority. Strength can increase the feminine power of the Empress and enhance her seductive and emotional side. The Devil can bring an uncomfortable, manipulative edge.

Inverted she becomes the Tyrant, a controlling and selfish mother.

"There's something about maternal love—it might just be the strongest human spiritual bond there is."

—THE FALL

IIII THE EMPEROR

The Emperor represents authority, stability, and law. He is not as concerned with justice as he is with keeping the social order—usually for good. In the classic tarots, the marriage between the Emperor and the Empress is clear as they display similar heraldic symbols. In Tarot del Toro, they both belong to the fairy realm, even though they come from different universes. The Emperor represented here is Balor, the elfin king from *Hellboy II*. For symbolic clarity, he is represented before he lost his arm.

The Emperor's actions are tied to the practical world, so he is shown resting on a rock. However, he is not a primitive being. Under his mantle, a tail slithers and holds a key: a symbol of being in control of what is "below"—the atavistic destructive instincts in all of us. The rock, or shield, he leans on shows the threatening figure of a Golden Army soldier: The Emperor does not need to embrace direct action, he only needs to show authority. His energy is mental, as the branches that grow from his head show.

Despite him being a mature character, perhaps an old man, green leaves sprout from his scepter, a sign of a vivifying power. As an archetypal father figure, he is also a promoter of life, although to a lesser extent than the Empress.

The presence of the Emperor in a reading always suggests power and authority, usually put at the service of order, prosperity, and security. The Emperor attracts the trust of family, friends, and associates. In short: He promotes stability and wealth for himself, and for others too. If he is accompanied by Justice, we can also underline his equanimity. With the World, his works can be especially fruitful. With the Sun, his followers will be filled with hope and joy. He can mount the Chariot to conquer new frontiers and widen his territories, but he is fearsome if he associates with the Devil, for he can become unpredictable and capricious.

When inverted, he is the Oppressor—despotic and materialistic; dogmatic and arrogant.

"But Captain, to obey, just like that, for obedience's sake . . . without questioning' . . . that's something' only people like you do."

—PAN'S LABYRINTH

V THE HIEROPHANT

If the Emperor controls the material world, the Hierophant is responsible for the spiritual realm. He relates to the High Priestess as the Emperor relates to the Empress. Both women have subtle, passive powers. Each, in her own way, is fertile. If the Emperor rules the world the Empress gives birth to, the Hierophant celebrates the secret rites the High Priestess imagines. If the Emperor writes the material law, the Hierophant rules the moral principles behind it. He is the bridge to the higher realms, to the divine—or spiritual— world. He is a priest, a mentor, a guru, a spiritual guide.

The Hierophant is always depicted as a hieratic and ominous figure, larger than the mortals who pray at his feet. Usually, the figure of a Christian pope is chosen for this card, but Tarot del Toro uses the Master, the supreme vampire of *The Strain*. The archetype of the one that can carry others to a supernatural life cannot be better represented than in the form of a vampire. Our Hierophant holds a scepter made of bones as a symbol of rebirth and dresses as a monk, according to his priestly condition. Mortals kneel before him and before the fire of revelation. The background reminds us that we are in a temple, the usual setting for the rituals of organized cults.

The Hierophant brings the deepest inspiration, the code of honor, and the rigidity of principles to our reading. He does not bring great material benefits, but he works wonders when spiritual and moral assistance is needed. He radiates an aura of elevation and purification. When combined with the Emperor, his authority may be too concentrated and overwhelming; with the Moon, he may show a somewhat dark and disturbing sectarian influence; with the Devil, he may indicate a false guide who is trying to take advantage of his privileged position. With the Sun, however, he is an enlightened counselor who can teach others.

Inverted, this card becomes the Inquisitor, who punishes any deviation from his strict and blindsided doctrine. His judgment is shortsighted and shallow. His faith, fanatical.

"It is not faith that distinguishes our real leaders. It is doubt. Their ability to overcome it."

—THE NIGHT ETERNAL

VI THE LOVERS

The Lovers' meaning has to do with choice, especially emotional choice. In many contexts, it can be even more focused and refer to crossroads of passion of any kind.

In the Tarot de Marseilles, the Lovers card is depicted as a man caught between two women. The exact situation here isn't clear: Are the women stalking the man or trying to embrace him? One appears to be innocent, while the other seems wicked. In Tarot del Toro, this duality is depicted by the characters from *The Shape of Water*, with their double nature, both human and aquatic. It is interesting to note the Mantegna deck illustrates this card with a figure of Venus in a marine environment.

The choices that the Lovers card forces us to make are mutually exclusive, so they always involve a sacrifice. The decision must be taken in the light of the truth that radiates from above. Below, the characters float in unstable equilibrium. There will be no rest until a decision is made.

The Lovers is not intrinsically a good or bad card. More than any other, its meaning depends on the cards around it. With the Wheel of Fortune, it signifies a particularly complex or shifting set of circumstances. With the Hermit, there are multiple possible meanings. If the Hermit appears before the Lovers, it shows us a situation in which the decision has to be made by a person on their own; if it appears afterward, it shows a decision that leads to loneliness. The Chariot adds a sense of urgency, and in the presence of the Hierophant, the decision could be blessed in the form of a marriage or contract. Conversely, if it is followed by the Tower, ruin and crisis loom. Beware if the Devil haunts the Lovers, for it could represent some temptation that affects the free decision of the interested party.

Inverted, the Lovers turns into the Entanglement. Hidden intentions, indecision, and wrong assessments cloud the situation. If we look at the card in this position, the light comes from below, so it loses its divine quality.

"But I can't be alone, can I? Of course not; I'm not that special. [. . .] What if you and I are not the last of our kinds, but one of the first? The first of better creatures in a better world? We can hope, can't we? That we're not of the past, but the future?"

—*The Shape of Water* (novelization)

VII THE CHARIOT

The Chariot signifies advance, action, and energy. He is autonomous and audacious. He moves forward in search of his destiny, guided only by his own criteria.

Traditional tarots represent different mythical characters for this card, but Tarot del Toro displays the unforgettable *Hellboy II* cart troll. This character supports the idea that the querent is on a journey propelled by his own power, as the crown and banner testify; enhanced by discipline, as shown by the arms tied to the wooden blocks the character uses to push himself forward; and containing his passions, which is why he is wrapped in a sack. He triumphs over difficulties: Even the supreme difficulty of lacking legs does not prevent him from proceeding. Although horses are a common element of this card, we must not forget that decks as old as Mantegna and Giovanni Vacchetta's do not include them. Our coachman carries a bell to announce his presence and some horseshoes that will bring him luck.

The Chariot's movement is almost unstoppable and runs in a clear direction—especially under the light of the Star; much less so under the empire of the Fool. It gets an additional dose of triumphant glory in the presence of the Emperor and a warm boost of vitality near the Empress. If Strength is on hand, the Chariot can be violent and overwhelming, and in the company of card XIII, it can lead to territories where we can forget who we are. If the Chariot advances under the Sun, any obstacle will be very easy to overcome.

Inverted it becomes the Daredevil, one who advances without discipline or control. His energy is fiercely dispersed, he takes absurd risks and even causes dangerous accidents that involve himself and others.

"A key piece of advice [. . .]: If a road is not presented, you build one."

—GUILLERMO DEL TORO,
GUILLERMO DEL TORO'S CABINET OF CURIOSITIES

VIII JUSTICE

Some tarot scholars think that the image of Justice as a female figure holding scales has to do with the goddess Maat. Ancient Egyptians believed that the souls of the deceased were weighed against a feather—provided by Maat—to decide their fate in the afterlife. Tarot del Toro focuses on this old funerary symbolism and uses the ghost of Edith's mother from *Crimson Peak* as the central figure.

Justice stares directly at us, hieratic, authoritarian, sitting on a solid throne, isolated by a thick veil. She is blind to outward appearances, and because of that, she sees everything. She enhances her dignity with a coronet of withered flowers. Her staff is also dry and twisted. Everything is immutable, perhaps inert.

Instead of the archetypal scales, she holds a tray with two skulls on it, their owners rendered equal in death, as everyone is equal at the moment of judgment. A raven, emissary from the spirit world, whispers words of wisdom to the judge, who holds a bouquet of flowers in her lap, a testimony to the benefits of her implacable nature, devoid of emotion and humanity.

Justice is a card of balance and equanimity, although in certain combinations it can lead to lack of action. In relation to emotions, it is a sign of indifference and coldness. With the Emperor, it speaks of civic devotion, and with the Hierophant, of a great respect for institutions and traditions that can manifest as fundamentalism when the card is reversed. The Empress brings a little empathy. If the Hanged is close, it speaks to an overly harsh verdict, especially if Strength is around. With the Devil, it can indicate an issue with a wrong set of values, thoughts, or expectations or an impostor posing as an authority.

Inverted, Justice becomes the avenger. Lacking feelings and empathy, she considers laws and traditions more important than people. In this position, she is capable of anything in order to maintain respect for the established codes and will act without any hint of passion.

"Man killing man, man helping man, both of them anonymous: the scourge and the blessing."

—*THE STRAIN* (GRAPHIC NOVEL)

VIIII THE HERMIT

The Hermit seeks the truth in the shadows. His quest is a spiritual one. In Guillermo's iconic fantasy movie *Pan's Labyrinth*, the monstrous Pale Man appears as one of the guises of the faun and one of the tests, like the toad that Ofelia must pass to return to the realm of the underworld. He is a perfect character to portray the Hermit: He has been blinded but sees again, like St. Paul. Like Odin and Horus, he sacrificed vision for knowledge. The symbolism of the mystical eye, which looks more to the spiritual world than to matter, is also present in the character's clothes.

The Hermit symbolizes self-knowledge, introspection, and the inner search. In an ideal situation, his state of isolation implies a great capacity for concentration and willpower, so it is a positive card when related to personal matters. Socially and financially, it indicates little need for relationships and material resources. His ideal partner is the Star, as she brings purpose to his search. Justice and Temperance balance his purpose and his clarity of mind—necessary for him and his quest. If he walks under the Sun, he may get distracted by the shiny outer world. If he walks under the Moon, he may receive the inspiration he needs, but he may become absorbed if the card appears reversed. With the Magician, he becomes an artist—perhaps obsessed—in search of the masterpiece, and with Judgement he becomes a wandering ronin. If he appears next to the Tower, it is important to know whether he is heading for ruin or running away from it. Finally, if he is related to the Hanged, he is disoriented, and his search may lead to the final confusion.

Inverted he becomes the Misanthrope, who lives in sterile solitude. He doesn't know what he is looking for, but he knows he needs to wander alone. He is often immersed in melancholy, insensitivity, and obsession.

"The most intelligent of creatures often make the fewest sounds."

—The Shape of Water

X THE WHEEL OF FORTUNE

The image of Fortune as a wheel dragging people through cycles of uneven luck is an ancient and powerful symbol. But it is about more than luck. It is also the wheel of birth and death, of reincarnation and the great cosmic cycle.

Tarot del Toro illustrates the Wheel of Fortune as the water mill from *Pan's Labyrinth*. The mill adds a layer of meaning to the wheel symbol: There is an ultimate purpose. Just as the mill transforms grain into flour, the cosmic wheel regenerates, channels, and harmonizes the energy of the universe. As in other tarot decks, there are three figures stretched out upon the wheel. One figure ascends with one hand raised upward. On the opposite side of the wheel, another figure descends, ready to dive into the river of blood beneath the wheel. At the top of the wheel, a third figure seems to be crowned with laurel leaves—the symbol of triumph—and holds a sickle, as if to harvest the fruits of the earth. But let's not fool ourselves, the three characters are one and the same: neither men nor women, neither young nor old, with no identity, no race, no defined features, imprisoned in an infinite circle of creation and destruction, of triumph and defeat, of splendor and misfortune.

The Wheel of Fortune is instability, unpredictability, and lack of control. Viewed more positively, it implies new opportunities. On the negative side, it implies shock and anxiety. It can speak of a certain chaos in the environment when it appears with the World, even of particular crises when it is accompanied by the Emperor (political issues), the Empress (family), or Justice (law). If the card appears under the Tower, we may be facing a radical rearrangement of the status quo. With the Lovers, emotional tensions are rising, and next to card XIII, without any doubt, the Wheel is coming to the end of a cycle.

The Wheel of Fortune does not change if it appears inverted, because the direction of its turn remains unchanged in any position.

"Stay by my side as I fade / so you can point to the end of my struggle / and the twilight of eternal days / at the low, dark edge of life."

—Translation of a fragment of "In Memoriam A.H.H." by Alfred, Lord Tennyson, in *The Devil's Backbone*

XI STRENGTH

Although today we are used to seeing Strength represented as a female figure, many ancient models of tarot reserved this card for figures such as Hercules or Samson. Tarot del Toro revives this old imagery and dedicates this card to the behemoth Mr. Wink, henchman to Prince Nuada in *Hellboy II* and the perfect character to represent unstoppable energy.

It should be noted that Strength does not characterize gross or blind physical power, but rather discipline and unstoppable will. The character's iron hand is an extraordinary symbol. Strength is a master of himself—his will and discipline are self-imposed, as evidenced by the broken chains attached to his leg. His wounds and bruises show the risks of taking on that responsibility, while the subjugated monster he has trapped with his massive hands represents his dominance over the base passions, the wild nature.

Nevertheless, the monstrous nature of the central figure—Mr. Wink here—indicates that, very often, Strength entails an excess, a lack of judgment, a certain degree of transgression and abuse.

Strength gives the other cards an extra boost of energy and drive. When it holds the leading role, the card speaks of efficiency of action and channeled passion. If it is accompanied by other high-energy cards, it speaks to the legitimacy of their aims, signifying triumph with the Emperor, approval with the Empress, and moral leadership with the Hierophant. But beware, Justice at its side can render this card ruthless, the Devil can make Strength turn into violence, and the Hanged can turn his power against himself.

If inverted, Strength turns into Brutality, suggesting violence and cruelty. It can speak of tyranny if escorted by the Emperor or of jealousy if tangential to the Lovers.

"Weakness is giving in to temptation. Strength is resisting it."

—*The Night Eternal*

XII THE HANGED

Throughout mythology, we see evidence of divine beings—Osiris, Odin, Christ—who were hanged to be reborn as superior beings. The Hanged symbolizes a person in the intermediate state of that process. Awaiting rebirth, he is nowhere, lost in his inner maze. In traditional cards, the Hanged hangs from a branch. However, since it is often said that the

Hanged dwells in limbo, Tarot del Toro depicts him as one of the fetuses preserved in liquor jars in *The Devil's Backbone*. If we analyze that movie, the parallels are even more remarkable, since in the film this liquor is called "limbo water" and the fetuses "nobody's children." It is interesting to note that many scholars of tarot speak of the Hanged in the same terms because it is in a state of latency. Although it is alive and conscious, it cannot act in the physical world because it is upside down and locked in its glass chrysalis. It can only do one thing: wait.

If the Hanged appears, we gain a clear sense of restriction, of being held, of waiting. Accompanied by cards like the Sun or the Star, it suggests a higher end and a bright outcome: the promised rebirth to a higher existence. Next to card XIII, he speaks of essential renewal, although if one is reversed there may be suffocation and metaphorical miscarriage. The Devil turns limbo into hell, and the World speaks of the gestation of good fruits, of the arrival of a new spring. Next to Judgement, it may reveal that the end of stagnation must come from external sources.

Inverted, the Hanged becomes the condemned, locked up against his will, hopeless, desperate about his lack of mobility.

"Feet are what connect you to the ground, and when you are poor, none of that ground belongs to you."

—*The Shape of Water* (novelization)

XIII

This card provides the most terrible and powerful vision in any tarot deck. Ruled by number XIII, of fatal reputation, this card usually shows a stark skeleton wielding a scythe over the remains of shattered corpses. In many classic tarot decks, this card does not have a name. This is an important clue for many scholars, who believe the old card creators eliminated it for a reason: They did not want to focus the meaning of it on death. They did not want XIII to be interpreted as a mere announcement of somebody's demise. In fact, the meaning of this arcana is much more open-ended and much less apocalyptic. It speaks of rebirth, renewal, and radical change. The scythe cuts the ripe fruits of the earth and prepares the field for spring. The old must die in order to give way to the new. The earth dies to be reborn.

Tarot del Toro relies—of course—on the Angel of Death from *Hellboy II* to represent this arcana. The wings reinforce the idea of transformation and change, and the head— blinded—suggests inevitability and equity of renewal.

XIII announces transformation. It can be a crisis of health, money, labor, or love. The accompanying cards will say so. These crises almost always come with benefits and sacrifices. The presence of the Lovers can speak of the end of one romance and the beginning of another; the Hermit, of a necessary, slow, and tortuous inner renewal; the Tower, a financial or work crisis; the World, the loss of confidence in one's surroundings. The Fool may imply liberation, while the Hanged may predict we are heading for damnation. In both cases, the new cycle is not a very promising one. On the contrary, the Sun close by produces an optimal result, as transmutation produces gold and brings us closer to perfection.

Inverted, card XIII denotes sterile and uncompensated loss, perhaps a process that ends without a solution.

"She forgot who she was and where she came from. Her body suffered cold, sickness, and pain. Eventually, she died."

—*Pan's Labyrinth*

XIIII TEMPERANCE

This card refers to the classic virtue of moderation. In Tarot del Toro, it is represented by a figure inspired by Edith Cushing from *Crimson Peak*. She is dressed in white and holds a lily, both symbols of purity and chastity. She has a serene stance despite being surrounded by flames. The wings that usually adorn her in the classic tarots have been removed, although they are suggested by elements of the dress, the hair, and the flames in the background.

Some traditional models—in fact, the best-known ones—present the figure of Temperance holding two jugs exchanging liquids. In our representation, these jugs are replaced by a lily, which maintains the characteristic dynamic shape. It could be thought that, after the passing brought on by card XIII, this arcana shows one of the plants cut down by the scythe, demonstrating that the harvest is complete and calm returns.

Temperance is, in a sense, the opposite of Strength: Instead of forceful dominance, it speaks of effortless—but no less effective—action. There is no struggle, but harmony, serenity, and subtlety, in both the spiritual or mental parts of life and in relationships with others. A certain lack of passion can be attributed to her, especially in the presence of the Moon. Perhaps she is too docile in the presence of Justice. She calms the wandering of the Fool and serenely tames the lower instincts of the Devil. She turns Strength into precise and concentrated energy, and therefore her actions become more effective. She slows down the Chariot and the Wheel of Fortune, which will be appreciated by those who ride one or the other.

If inverted, she becomes the Coward, who avoids all conflict and never acts, blocked by pure and simple fear.

"... down here, hate has no purpose. Down here, you embrace your foes until they become your friends. Down here, you seek not to be one being', but all being's, and all at once [...] She is full. She is perfect."

—*The Shape of Water* (novelization)

XV THE DEVIL

The Devil is the ancient, chaotic, and feral god present in religions since time immemorial. He resembles, above all, the Christian devil, inspired by old horned gods, especially the faun Pan, from whose name the word panic is derived. Needless to say, in Tarot del Toro, the Devil is inspired by Hellboy, the wonderful character created by Mike Mignola and brought to the screen twice by Guillermo.

Our Devil is strong and red. Each leg is different, as in many old traditions, and he wears a face on his belly that symbolizes the dictatorship of his base appetites. His wings are too small for flying, and his hand of stone seems an additional burden that anchors him to the earthly world or even to "the world below," where he is the undisputed king, with his crown and his slaves. He wields a sword of fire in his left hand. It is not a sword that defends the law but one that destroys with the implacable force of instinct and savagery.

The Devil is only evil in the eyes of men. In reality, he is an irrational, unbridled, atavistic, and amoral force. The card's appearance in a spread takes us to that territory where law, reason, and morality succumb to the empire of passion, appetite, and pure unleashed will. If the Devil is handling the Chariot, his action will be fearsome and unstoppable. It is advisable to stay out of his way. With the Hanged by his side, his appetites turn against him, hinting at debilitating addictions or limitations due to a lack of self-control. The Moon can twist his intentions with perversity, while the Sun can turn him into a mischievous and even amusing faun. The Magician can give him a way to sublimate his energies through creativity, although his works will always have a disturbing or unsettling nuance.

Inverted, he is Lucifer, the fallen angel, the enemy of God. His energy is even more intense, destructive, and furious.

"To learn what we fear is to learn who we are."

—Guillermo del Toro

XVI THE TOWER

This arcana immediately suggests the Tower of Babel, a monument to human pride destroyed by the wrath of God. In Tarot del Toro, the Tower is both a scene and a character, inspired by Cathedral Head, one of the secondary characters in *Hellboy II*. This character is appropriate because the Tower, from a symbolic point of view, has to be understood as the deepest structure of the individual. And this structure is formed by elements of his environment—family, friends, work, institutions—and also by his own being.

The Tower is struck by a bolt of energy from above, and its appearance is a punishment that calls for rectification. Although the building is partly damaged, the base remains unchanged: It is possible to rebuild the whole structure. In traditional decks, two figures fall from the tower. In Tarot del Toro, these figures appear embroidered on the character's dress.

The presence of the Tower means disaster, unforeseen accidents. It can rarely be interpreted in a positive way. In the best case, such as when the Sun shines or the Fool walks away, it can represent the demolition of outdated structures and liberation from an oppressive environment. Temperance is a good adviser when the floor rumbles, and we will need her prudent counsel, hopefully with the guidance of the Star. The Chariot should not head for the center of the hurricane, although it may be useful for us to get away from it. If the Devil is nearby, we can think of unknown agents and conspiracies. Card XIII has an ambiguous meaning because it indicates a deeper trauma but a more radical renewal. And this can be liberating or healing.

Inverted, the Tower becomes the Ruin. The structure sustains more damage, and rebuilding is harder. If the Fool is near, it may symbolize the need to start again from scratch in another place.

"There are things you can't fight—acts of God. You see a hurricane coming, you get out of the way."

—PACIFIC RIM

XVII THE STAR

A maiden kneels under the stars. She is submissive to the cosmic order and receptive to its energy. One star rules the whole image and seven smaller ones surround her in harmony. There are seven virtues, seven planets known in the classical era, seven days of the week, seven chakras, seven alchemical metals, and seven steps of transformation. There are seven colors in the rainbow. The world was created in seven days in the creation myth of both Judaism and Christianity. For many traditions and teachings, seven is a number of totality and perfection.

In the best-known tarot decks, the Star shows a naked maiden pouring water from two jugs into a river or pond. We can feel a connection between that action and the energy of the stars. For Tarot del Toro, Ofelia, the main character of *Pan's Labyrinth*, has been chosen to represent this lovely card. She has dropped the jugs and is holding a book while fairies flutter around her. It seems that her work is done. Ethereal energy is vividly manifesting itself through a naive, childish, carefree—and therefore deeply powerful—character.

The Star is always a happy card in a tarot reading. Under the Star's rule, everything takes its rightful place in the order of the universe. To find our true objective, we must accept her guidance. With the Empress, it acquires a certain sensual character that may attract others to the right path. With the Lovers, it guarantees a balanced and mutual romantic relationship. If the Emperor is placed under its light, we can glimpse a triumph that does not take advantage of others and that will bring lasting satisfaction. The Star leads the Chariot to a good destiny, inspires Justice, and puts an end to the Fool's wandering by turning him into another archetype that will follow a clear path. It gives a practical sense to the Magician and a very convenient anchor to the inner mazes that the Moon may present.

Inverted, she becomes the Mirage and can guide us deep into the desert through illusory appearances and superficial claims. With the Magician, she may indicate a tendency toward exhibitionism and with the Moon, great insecurity.

"When I was a kid, whenever I'd feel small or lonely, I'd look up at the stars."

—Pacific Rim

XVIII THE MOON

The Moon card is usually divided into three levels. In the upper level, the Moon looks down toward the Earth, shedding droplets of color to show her influence. In the middle level, a figure or set of figures—a lady, some animals, or some astrologers, depending on the model—point toward her. The lower level usually includes a pool, a lake, or another humid cavity inhabited by an aquatic being.

Tarot del Toro retains the essence of these elements—the three levels, the moon, the dogs, the aquatic creature—and contextualizes them in the world of *Pan's Labyrinth*. The main addition is the tree that grows over the burrow of the giant toad, which here replaces the traditional crab. These changes are appropriate to the traditional meaning of the card, which marks an ascending energy from the aquatic or primeval through the earthly or animal to the celestial or transcendental. The tree underlines this vertical drive, but some of its branches twist toward the ground, indicating the possibility of this process becoming stagnant, since blockage and obsession are the least pleasant characteristics of this arcana.

The deepest meaning of the Moon has to do with purification and inner sublimation—processes that happen passively, without external action. Next to the Sun, the results are excellent, and these obscure processes provide luminous results. With the Hanged, however, it can indicate too much focus on the inner self, which can become unhealthy and obsessive. With the Tower, we can suspect the need to deal with an unpleasant inner reality. With the Hermit arises the possibility of a painful and—if reversed—unnecessary isolation. Together with the Devil she can indicate submission to a harmful figure. We hope that the Star or Temperance will provide guidance and strength of mind to this arcana to climb to higher grounds.

If inverted, the Moon is obscured and the Dark Night of the Soul begins. Disorientation grabs us and willpower disappears. It is not a good time for the Tower to fall apart or for the Devil to come and tempt us with addiction or destructive behavior.

"The moon will be full in three days. Your spirit shall forever remain among the humans. You shall age like them, you shall die like them, and all memory of you shall fade in time."

—PAN'S LABYRINTH

XVIIII THE SUN

The Sun is the universal symbol of rebirth and therefore of immortality. Tarot del Toro merges two classic representations of this card that resonate with that symbolism. The first and best known features the Sun shining over a pair of embraced twins; the second, more archaic, depicts the Sun blessing a hero or champion by shining on one of his hands, over his head, or from his chest.

It is fascinating how the symbols intertwine in ways beyond our control. The initial inspiration for this card was the model of a hero with the Sun on his chest. Gipsy Danger, the lead Jaeger in *Pacific Rim*, was chosen for the role because of its burning power core, clearly shown in the movie. Then, surprisingly, the discarded motif of the embracing twins surfaced again, as the only way to handle the overwhelming energy of the titan is through the linked minds of two closely bonded pilots. There is no such thing as coincidence when it comes to symbols.

The Sun dispels the shadows, literally and metaphorically, bringing clear vision. The intimate, wet, silent, cold illumination that the Moon stimulates has nothing to do with the Sun's path, which enlightens through an external, communicative, and warm process.

The Sun floods its surroundings with benevolence, vitality, and openness. It enhances the motherhood of the Empress and makes the Emperor and Justice benevolent. It opens horizons for the Chariot and clears the path for the Fool, who may behave like a merry buffoon or like a swift traveler. The Hermit can put out his lantern for a while and hopefully—especially with the help of the Star—find what he is looking for in the dark. Everything grows under the Sun's rule, though its light, if enhanced by Strength, may disturb some.

Inverted, the Sun becomes the Blinding Light. Its glow can hide the truth, and its heat can burn, especially if the Devil is around. Confusion will spread with the Hanged, and anger will arise in the presence of Strength.

"Night is not an absence of light, but in fact, it is daytime that is a brief respite from the looming darkness . . ."

—*The Strain*

XX JUDGEMENT

In Guillermo's work, we find terrible threats rising from the afterlife, from other dimensions, from government offices, or even from the heart of the forests of our imagination. But perhaps the most powerful apocalyptic image in his filmography is the enormous rusty bomb stuck in the middle of the orphanage yard in *The Devil's Backbone*. That image is a clear indicator of impending trial in the film, and in Tarot del Toro, it replaces the usual angel who plays the trumpet of the Apocalypse. At the bottom, according to the traditional representation, the dead arise in an attitude of prayer.

This card refers to a very specific situation: a time for evaluation. It indicates that the moment has come to review our plans as well as our objectives and habits. It does not offer the inevitable renewal of card XIII or warn of the unexpected catastrophe of the Tower. Rather, it is a sign that we must consciously analyze our situation and decide whether it is best to continue, to stop, or to change our way.

Along with the Fool, it means we need to drop acquired yokes; with Justice, it brings an accurate verdict. It is benevolent with the Empress or severe with the Hierophant. If the Tower appears, the sentence will be a shock. Proximity of card XIII implies our everyday world—family, work, friends—can be annihilated if we judge severely. With the Devil, we may be judged by others. Judgement combines happily with Temperance, which balances and moderates the verdict, and with the High Priestess and the Star, which can provide, respectively, wisdom and a set of bright references.

Inverted, Judgement turns into Condemnation, and her verdict, whether it comes from us or from others, can be harsh and adverse. We do not want the Hermit or the Hanged around, for they would realize that sentence in the form of isolation or incapacity.

"This is what the beginning of the end of the world will look like."

—*The Strain*

XXI THE WORLD

Almost every tarot deck depicts this arcana as a wheel or a mandorla that encloses a human figure. It is the last of the arcana and symbolizes the fulfillment of the process the Fool started at the beginning of the journey. Tarot del Toro maintains the oval and symmetrical composition of the classic card design but approaches its meaning with imagery paying homage to Guillermo's film *Mimic*, replacing the human character with a chrysalis at the moment of opening. The image maintains its symbolism: The potential becomes real, the evolution has been completed, the work is now finished, and it is perfect.

The World is a very positive card that improves any spread. When it appears, the flowering of all the inner processes and the fruition of the outer ones takes place. The disparate elements are unified, the merits are recognized, the efforts are rewarded, the world around us widens. For the Fool, it is rest after finding his grail; for the Magician, it is the culmination of his masterwork. For the High Priestess, it is the revelation of the great secret. For the Emperor, the conquest and pacification of his "territories," where people will live in order and, with the help of the Empress, be happy and satisfied. We can only hope the Sun will shine so the World's gifts will be infinite.

Inverted, this card becomes the Mundane. When it appears, we fear that the radiant energy of the world will distract us from our center and take us away from our innermost circle—our family and friends. This is enhanced in the presence of the enthusiastic Chariot, the unstable Fool, and the tempting Devil.

"The butterfly does not look back upon its caterpillar self, either fondly or wistfully; it simply flies on."

—THE NIGHT ETERNAL

THE MINOR ARCANA

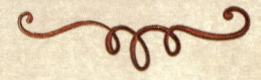

The Minor Arcana consists of fifty-six cards, grouped into four sets of fourteen. The first cards of each set are numbered one (ace) to ten, and the last four depict courtly characters: king, queen, knight, and valet. These sets are called suits, and each one is dedicated to a different symbol: Blades, Goblets, Wands, and Discs. The names of these suits vary from deck to deck and from scholar to scholar. Our choices are based on what seems to fit best with Guillermo's mythology.

Some tarot readers put aside the Minor Arcana and use only the major cards. Others include them but believe they provide only secondary information—a complement to the Major Arcana. A third group gives both kinds of cards the same importance. You must study them and decide for yourself how you will act. A very common recommendation is to make your first readings with Major Arcana only, and wait to incorporate the minor once your skills are established. As always with tarot, your intuition has to mark your way.

THE SUITS AND THE COURTLY FIGURES

There is an intimate relationship between each of the suits and each of the courtly figures.

The king cards and suit of Wands are both ruled by the element of fire. They are energetic and transformative. Wands—also called Clubs, Batons, Stoves, or Rods—are incarnations of the magic wand of fairy tales, Hermes's caduceus, and the mandrake.

The queen cards and suit of Goblets—also called Cups or Chalices—are ruled by water. They express the power of the grail, fluidity, fecundity, the emotional.

The knight cards and suit of Blades—or Swords—are ruled by air. They represent movement, agility, and maybe violence. Excalibur, Andúril, Durendal are notable incarnations of Blades in mythology.

The valet cards and suit of Discs—also called Pentacles, Coins, or Rings—are ruled by earth and linked to everything that is practical and material, like money.

Attention must be paid when courtly figures match their dominant suit symbol. The king of Wands, the queen of Goblets, the knight of Blades, and the valet of Discs are twice infused with the same meaning. Thus, the king of Wands is doubly fiery, authoritarian, and powerful; the queen of Goblets is especially sensitive and fertile; the knight of Blades is the most dynamic and belligerent of his class; and the valet of Discs stands out for his materialism and practicality. It is easy to infer the other figure and suit combinations, taking into account the suit meaning is an accessory to that of the figure.

THE COURT CARDS INTERPRETED

King of Wands: fire matched with fire. Exalted action. Great power. Unleashed activity. Unlimited possibilities of creation. If it appears inverted, it indicates excessive strength, perhaps abuse and tyranny. His incarnation in Tarot del Toro is the king of the underworld from *Pan's Labyrinth*.

Queen of Wands: water heated by fire. Transformation through loving contemplation. Fertility. Affectionate leadership. Sensuality and empathy. Inverted, it can speak of vanity and manipulative sensuality. We meet here an ambiguous fairy princess, who may have dwelled in the underworld realms of *Pan's Labyrinth* or *Hellboy II*.

Knight of Wands: air warmed by fire. The summer breeze. We could say that the activity and dynamism of air prevails over the transformative capacity of fire. It speaks of inspirational power and the ability to help. When inverted, it indicates the dispersion of energies, likely due to an excess of aims and interests. We find here an insect and a fairy, which are one and the same in *Pan's Labyrinth*.

Valet of Wands: earth melted by fire. As lava or molten metals, it is ductile and adaptable. It implies creativity and an artistic attitude. If it appears inverted, it indicates a probable lack of focus or an unclear objective. A crow guard from *Hellboy II* is represented in this card.

King of Goblets: Water mitigates the flames. Kind, empathic use of power. Magnanimity. If inverted, we have perhaps found a twisted leader or a dark father, as evil as the vampire from *The Strain* who this card depicts.

Queen of Goblets: Water doubles water. Clear thoughts, intentions, and feelings. If it appears inverted, it means these calm waters are delusive, and we can drown in them. The idea for this card was inspired by *The Strain*.

Knight of Goblets: Wind agitates water. Our emotional world will shake. We must prepare our hearts for changes. If the card appears upright, we can expect a positive outcome; if inverted, the changes will involve suffering. This card, in Tarot del Toro, uses the idea of the corpse that has to be carried to its proper place—an image taken from *Hellboy*.

Valet of Goblets: humid soil. This card speaks of troubled growth, of development that seldom brings an abundant harvest. Uncertain and risky result. If the card appears inverted, it may mean that dark offshoots are sprawling, sucking the aliment from the ground (as *The Strain* vampire in the card shows), and that the fruits of the process will be unfortunate.

King of Blades: The fire roars when enlivened by the air. Authority and dynamism combined. Intelligence and power. Genius and authority. Transformative mental energy, but a lack of empathy. If it appears inverted, these last features are accentuated, and in the presence of the Devil, for example, it may become truly cruel. We have chosen for this card an allegorical figure of death, a sort of male counterpart to the Angel of Death from *Hellboy II*.

Queen of Blades: humid air. Mist. Emotional futility. Movement based only on feelings. Uncontrolled changes. Shortsightedness. These qualities are aggravated if the card appears inverted. This card is represented by a figure that is a medievalized interpretation of a beheaded *Strain* vampire.

Knight of Blades: air matched with air. Unleashed, sterile action. Without emotion, roots, or creativity, action is just senseless movement. It can be elegant and beautiful but also dangerous and disorienting (especially if the card appears inverted). Karl Ruprect Kroenen, from *Hellboy*, is depicted on this card.

Valet of Blades: the air that blows over a fertile earth. This card represents the power of invention and the growth that comes from the combination of a great scope and a honed practical sense. It can imply a certain incompatibility of objectives and possibilities if it appears inverted. The card depicts Mercedes, Captain Vidal's housekeeper and Ofelia's friend in *Pan's Labyrinth*.

King of Discs: burning rock. Coal. Shiny metals. Financial wealth and power. When inverted, it can imply greed and materialism. The card is illustrated with a Golden Army soldier from *Hellboy II*.

Queen of Discs: Water soaks the earth. Mud. A passion for the earthly, a desire for riches and material goods that can void materialism when the card appears inverted. A Judas breed roach from *Mimic* appears in this card.

Knight of Discs: the dust cloud. The material world in action. It indicates financial transactions, money (or material goods or properties) changing hands. The position (upright or inverted) tells if those changes are favorable or not. A medievalized version of Striker Eureka from *Pacific Rim* fights its Kaiju counterpart Knifehead on this card.

Valet of Discs: the earth below the earth. Extreme materialism, sharpened practicality. Perhaps vulgarity and shortsightedness if the card appears inverted. Cherno Alpha, another Jaeger from *Pacific Rim*, illustrates this card.

NUMERICAL CARDS

When interpreting the numerical cards, we must combine the symbolism of the suits, which we already know, with the meaning of each of the numbers. These meanings can be highly subjective (as can everything in tarot!) and oftentimes differ according to the reader's tradition or instinct. It is up to you to bring your intuition to bear and interpret the numbers in a way that feels right. That being said, many interpretations follow the basic narrative structure you find below. These meanings represent a complete story cycle, with several paths emerging in the second half.

1: Origin. The first step, the seed, the cell, potentiality.
2: Tension. A new element appears, and naturally, confrontation arises.
3: Fruits. This tension is alleviated when a third element is generated.
4: Stability. Equilibrium is restored.
5: Conflict. Equilibrium disappears again for a long time.
6: Frustration. We are unable to cope with the conflict that has just started.
7: Triumph. The perfect number witnesses our victory.
8: Defeat. We have been defeated in the conflict.
9: Happy ending of the process. Harvest.
10: Sterile closure of the process.

Some examples. Needless to say, the inverted position indicates the reduction of the positive aspects and the aggravation of the negative ones.

> Ace of Goblets: incubation of new feelings, or a real pregnancy
>
> Ace of Discs: the first coin a fortune will be built upon
>
> Two of Blades: rivalry with a competitor
>
> Three of Discs: possible gains after a trial or some kind of risky business
>
> Four of Goblets: monotony in a relationship
>
> Five of Blades: double jeopardy—the most undesirable Minor Arcana, which becomes especially harmful in the presence of card XIII, the Devil, or the Tower
>
> Six of Wands: unfinished business due to laziness or fear
>
> Seven of Blades: victory over an enemy
>
> Eight of Discs: possible bankruptcy, major money losses
>
> Nine of Wands: professional success, creation of a masterpiece
>
> Ten of Wands: permanent loss of energy or authority

READINGS

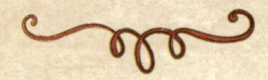

Whether you believe in magic or in the power of symbols; whether you are attempting to predict the future or to know yourself better; or even if you are only dreaming stories, you need a structure that allows you to organize and interpret the information in the cards. We call these methods of organization spreads. The reading of the cards may be a solitary experience—or may occur between a tarot reader and a querent. In both cases, it is best to perform the readings in an intimate and quiet place. More esoteric people may add ritual elements to the reading, such as meditation, energy charging, and cleansing, however this is entirely optional and something to explore on your own.

The following is an explanation of a reading method used by Don Miguel. There are many other methods, some simpler and others infinitely more complex, however I have always found this spread to be highly accessible. It is a good spread for beginner readers and experienced readers alike. It can be practiced with the whole deck, however for the sake of ease we will use only the Major Arcana in the examples.

DON MIGUEL'S CROSS METHOD

The reader shuffles the cards and places them on the table. The querent—or the reader themselves if this is a solo reading—cuts the deck. The reader turns the top half upside down in order to ensure that some cards can appear inverted, then reshuffles.

The reader asks the querent to choose four numbers between one and twenty-two. Starting at the top of the deck, the reader counts down twenty-two cards, removes those cards that correspond to the numbers the querent selected, and places them in the following pattern:

```
                    Card 3
        Card 2              Card 1
                    Card 4
```

The numbers in the diagram above represent the order of the cards pulled. Next, the values of the cards are added. If the result is greater than eighteen, the two resulting digits are added together. If any court cards are present, they will correspond to the numbers 11 through 14, starting with the valet: valet (11), knight (12), queen (13), king (14).

Example: four cards are drawn: XVI (The Tower), XIII, VIII (Justice), and II (The High Priestess). So, 16 + 13 + 8 + 2 = 39. As the number obtained is higher than 18, we break up that number, and then add up again: 3 + 9 = 12.

The reader then draws a final card by starting from the top of the deck, counting down the number of cards using the sum from the previous draws, and pulling that card.

This card goes in the center of the spread. The final pattern for our example would look like this:

Card 3 - VIII Justice

Card 2 - XIII   **Card 5 - XII The Hanged**   **Card 1 - XVI The Tower**

Card 4 - II The High Priestess

The deck with the remaining cards is set aside. If a card does not offer a clear reading and we need additional information, we will draw cards from the top of the deck for further information. The cards should be read according to the general meanings expressed in the table below and in this order: 5, 1, 2, 3, 4.

	3 WHAT THE QUERENT IS DOING NOW. Their present line of action.	
2 WHAT IS AGAINST US. Enemies, flaws, obstacles.	**5 THE QUERENT.** Who is he/she in this moment?	**1 WHAT FAVORS US.** Allies, virtues, opportunities.
	4 OUTPUT What we can expect if factors remain this way.	Reserve deck. In case of unclear readings, we can freely add cards to any position until meaning is clear.

THREE REAL READINGS
First Reading

VIIII - THE HERMIT

XV - THE DEVIL +	VII - THE CHARIOT	I - THE MAGICIAN
IIII - THE EMPEROR	(INVERTED) +	
(INVERTED)	XII - THE HANGED	
	(INVERTED)	

THE FOOL +
XVIIII - THE SUN

Don Miguel performed this reading for a young musician. The order of appearance of the cards was: I (The Magician), XV (The Devil), VIIII (The Hermit), and finally the card without a number (The Fool). The numbers were added (1 + 15 + 9 + 0) and, because the result (25) was higher than 18, it was broken up and added again, so Don Miguel extracted the seventh card down from the deck. It was the Chariot, inverted. This card was placed in the center of the spread.

The central card, the Chariot, inverted, seemed to express that the querent was experiencing a certain loss of direction. Don Miguel asked if that was the reason for the consultation, which the young man confirmed: He was having problems with his career. Interested in further information, Don Miguel extracted a complementary card from the deck. The Hanged (inverted) appeared, which showed the querent was depressed, blocked, or uninspired. This was also confirmed by the querent. The Magician on the right clearly expressed that his skills and artistic talents could be used to his advantage, but the Devil, in the position of difficulties, seemed to be a manifestation of a negative and ill-intentioned influence. Don Miguel wanted to know more and pulled out another card: the Emperor upside down. In combination with the Devil, it spoke of an authority figure with bad intentions as the source of the artist's stagnation. The young musician declared it was undoubtedly his instructor, with whom he had a difficult relationship. The top square housed the Hermit, so the current course of action seemed to point to isolation. Don Miguel and the young man agreed this strategy indicated the future distancing from the abusive tutor. The final card completed the story. The Fool and the Sun appeared in the lower square, predicting the outcome: The young artist would be happily freed.

Second Reading

XIIII - TEMPERANCE
(INVERTED)

VII - THE CHARIOT   I - THE MAGICIAN   THE FOOL
(INVERTED)   (INVERTED)

XVI - THE TOWER +
XIII

Don Miguel performed this reading for a woman in the middle of a crisis with her job. Symbolizing herself, the Magician appeared (inverted), suggesting the idea of sterile work and, probably, negligence in her performance, which the woman justified as lack of motivation. The Fool, in the box on the right, confronted with the Chariot (inverted) in the one on the left, supported this interpretation. She had in her favor the scattered and erratic energy of the Fool, which might alleviate her suffering to a degree, but would not be seen in a positive light by her bosses. The wild forces of a misdirected Chariot appeared as an obstacle, probably symbolizing contradictory orders from her superiors, who were likely fed up with her lack of commitment. The forecast was not very optimistic, and it seemed the querent was completely lost. Temperance appeared above, in the box that expresses the present dominant line of action. It was inverted, indicating passivity. The client agreed, as she didn't think anything could be done to resolve the matter. The lower box confirmed the bad outcome, as the Tower signaled an imminent breakdown. It was possible that the woman would soon lose her job if her attitude did not change. Both she and Don Miguel wanted to know more about it, so another card was taken from the deck: card XIII, which completed the meaning. For this woman, a cycle was coming to an end. It seemed clear that she would either get a new job soon or, perhaps, join the ranks of the unemployed.

Third Reading

*This reading is an example of how this spread can function using the full deck.

	10 OF DISCS	
	THE FOOL	

XX - JUDGEMENT	XVIII - THE MOON	III - THE EMPRESS
6 OF GOBLETS		

XII - THE HANGED

Don Miguel performed this reading for a mature woman who claimed to feel let down by life and a little depressed. There had been a lot of changes in her life lately (she did not specify what they were), and she was definitely not happy. The square of her present self, occupied by the Moon, was almost self-explanatory: She was in the process of accepting a new situation and needed to sublimate her energy. The other cards would tell more about how the process would develop. As her main helping force, the Empress appeared, and Don Miguel interpreted that motherhood was the most important thing in her life, perhaps the task she embraced with most devotion. This observation seemed to cause a deep emotional response in the woman. Against her, in the left square, Judgement showed up, and Don Miguel took another card to complete its meaning: It was the moment for a radical revision of her priorities, particularly those creating emotional frustration in her life, as Goblets point toward the world of emotions and number six has to do with frustration. Don Miguel asked the woman whether, perhaps, she was having problems with her sons. She confirmed this point but refused to tell more.

Don Miguel's attention then moved to the upper square, which indicates the present line of action of the querent. The ten of Discs spoke to materialism and impasse. In conjunction with the Fool, it suggested an attitude of neglect and a refusal to confront issues considered forever lost. The Hanged filled the lower square with a logical conclusion: If her problems were not confronted, the impasse would never end.

(After this reading, the woman explained that her sons had recently left the family home and that she felt "empty and useless," so she spent hours watching TV trying to not feel "sad and desperate.")

FINAL WORD

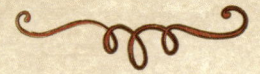

As you have realized, this guide is designed in an open and suggestive way and tries to avoid rigid systems and closed meanings. It intentionally avoids exploring each combination, and it is up to you to explore and reveal each shadowy corner of this art.

Tarot del Toro has been conceived as a first spark that hopefully triggers your interest in this old and mysterious game. Handle the cards, look at them for a long time, open your mind to their symbols, decipher what they tell you specifically, and invent your own codes. Explore other decks of cards. Try out other reading methods. Sometimes the cards will be opaque, and sometimes they will speak so clearly that you will be tempted to believe—if you don't already—in magic. The path of tarot is unique for each person. Walking it is a worthwhile experience.

"You have to believe the magic to see it."

—Guillermo del Toro

ABOUT GUILLERMO DEL TORO

Guillermo del Toro is the acclaimed director of *Pan's Labyrinth*, *Hellboy*, *Pacific Rim*, *Crimson Peak*, and *The Shape of Water*, for which he won the Academy Awards for Best Picture and Best Director. His Strain novels are international best sellers. He lives in Los Angeles.

ABOUT TOMÁS HIJO

Tomás Hijo is an illustrator, printmaker, and a professor of illustration at the University of Salamanca in Spain. He has illustrated more than seventy books and written ten of them, most of which are related to legends and folklore. He is the creator of the Nictonomicon, a collection of prints inspired by H. P. Lovecraft and a frequent collaborator with well-known Spanish radio and TV shows about Forteana and paranormal phenomena. Hijo received the Best Artwork Award from the Tolkien Society in 2015 in recognition of his works about J. R. R. Tolkien's books.

This is for Guillermo, who I felt was a friend even before I met him.

 Thanks to Elena, who cared.
 Thanks to Arturo, who inspired.
 Thanks to Don Miguel, who taught.
 Thanks to Sue, who helped.

TITAN
BOOKS

144 Southwark Street
London SE1 0UP
www.titanbooks.com

- Find us on Facebook: www.facebook.com/titanbooks
- Follow us on Twitter: @TitanBooks

Text © 2020 Tomás Hijo
Illustrations © 2020 Tomás Hijo
Foreword © 2020 Guillermo del Toro

All rights reserved. Published by Titan Books, London, in 2020.

Published by arrangement with Insight Editions, PO Box 3088, San Rafael, CA, 94912, USA. www.insighteditions.com

No part of this book may be reproduced, stored in a retrieval system, or transmitted, in any form or by any means without the prior written permission of the publisher, nor be otherwise circulated in any form of binding or cover other than that in which it is published and without a similar condition being imposed on the subsequent purchaser.

A CIP Catalogue record for this title is available from the British Library.

ISBN: 978-1-78909-647-7

ROOTS of PEACE   REPLANTED PAPER

Manufactured in China by Insight Editions

10 9 8 7 6 5 4